U.S. HISTORY IN REVIEW

The French and Indian War

BY KATHRYN WALTON

Enslow PUBLISHING

Please visit our website, www.enslow.com. For a free color catalog of all our high-quality books, call toll free 1-800-398-2504 or fax 1-877-980-4454.

Library of Congress Cataloging-in-Publication Data
Names: Walton, Kathryn, 1993- author.
Title: The French and Indian War / Kathryn Walton.
Description: Buffalo, New York : Enslow Publishing, [2024] | Series: U.S. history in review | Includes bibliographical references and index.
Identifiers: LCCN 2023003398 (print) | LCCN 2023003399 (ebook) | ISBN 9781978536159 (library binding) | ISBN 9781978536142 (paperback) | ISBN 9781978536166 (ebook)
Subjects: LCSH: United States–History–French and Indian War, 1754-1763–Juvenile literature.
Classification: LCC E199 .W2353 2024 (print) | LCC E199 (ebook) | DDC 973.2/6–dc23/eng/20230125
LC record available at https://lccn.loc.gov/2023003398
LC ebook record available at https://lccn.loc.gov/2023003399

Published in 2024 by
Enslow Publishing
2544 Clinton Street
Buffalo, NY 14224

Portions of this work were originally authored by Seth Lynch and published as *The French and Indian War.* All new material in this edition authored by Kathryn Walton.

Designer: Leslie Taylor
Editor: Natalie Humphrey

Photo credits: Cover Granger Collection/https://commons.wikimedia.org/wiki/File:Pontiac_in_1763.jpg; series art (grunge flag) Andrey Kuzmin/Shutterstock.com; series art (stamp icon) Stocker_team/Shutterstock.com; series art (font) santstock/Shutterstock.com; p. 5 Pinpin/https://commons.wikimedia.org/wiki/File:Nouvelle-France_map-en.svg; p. 7 RozenskiP/Shutterstock.com; p. 8 Sébastien Paquin/https://commons.wikimedia.org/wiki/File:Fort_Duquesne.jpg; p. 9 duncan1890/iStockphoto.com; p. 11 Washington-Custis-Lee Collection/https://commons.wikimedia.org/wiki/File:Washington_1772.jpg; p. 13 https://commons.wikimedia.org/wiki/File:Our_greater_country;_being_a_standard_history_of_the_United_States_from_the_discovery_of_the_American_coninent_to_the_present_time_(1901)_(14598200099).jpg; p. 15 Henry Alexander Ogden/https://commons.wikimedia.org/wiki/File:The_Victory_of_Montcalms_Troops_at_Carillon_by_Henry_Alexander_Ogden.JPG; p. 16 Manuela Michailescu/https://commons.wikimedia.org/wiki/File:Fort_Ticonderoga_cannon_detail.jpg; p, 17 tokar/Shutterstock.com; p. 19 Library of the Canadian Department of National Defence/https://commons.wikimedia.org/wiki/File:PlainsOfAbraham2007.jpg; p. 20 Sammy33/Shutterstock.com; p. 21 Blaue Max/https://commons.wikimedia.org/wiki/File:Seven_Years%27_War_Collage.jpg; p. 23 (Charles III and Louis XV) Morphart Creation/Shutterstock.com; p. 25 Rijksmuseum/https://commons.wikimedia.org/wiki/File:Allegorie op de Vrede van Parijs Paix rendue à l'Europe (titel op object) Pax Europae Reddita (titel op object), RP-P-1928-204 (cropped).jpg; p. 26 Simon Dannhauer/Shutterstock.com; p. 27 Alexander Lukatskiy/Shutterstock.com; p. 29 Fotokvadrat/Shutterstock.com.

Printed in the United States of America

CPSIA compliance information: Batch #CSENS24: For further information, contact Enslow Publishing at 1-800-398-2504.

Contents

Tension Grows 4
Claiming North America 6
The Battle of Jumonville Glen 10
Native Americans Help 12
The Seven Years' War 14
Capturing Canada 18
The Family Compact 22
The Treaty of Paris 24
Start of Revolution 28
Timeline 30
Glossary 31
For More Information 32
Index 32

*Words in the glossary appear in **bold** the first time they are used in the text.*

Tension Grows

By the 1750s, three countries claimed large parts of North America. Great Britain, France, and Spain each wanted to control the most land. No country would let go of its land without a fight. This growing **tension** partly caused the French and Indian War.

Learn More

European settlers acted as if they were moving into new land. But they weren't the first people in the Americas. Native peoples had lived and farmed in these areas for thousands of years.

North America, about 1750

Claiming North America

Along the East Coast of North America, Great Britain held 13 **colonies**. New France included part of what is now Canada and some lands along the Mississippi River as far south as Louisiana. Both countries claimed land near Lake Ontario and Ohio, also called the Ohio River valley.

Learn More

Spain also had claims to land in North America. The country claimed Florida, present-day Texas, California, New Mexico, and Mexico.

Ohio River valley

British colonists, wanting to spread west of the colonies, began moving onto land claimed by the French. By 1754, France had started building a **fort** in present-day Pennsylvania. This was on land the British also felt they had claimed.

model of Fort Duquesne

Fort Duquesne

Learn More

French forces also captured, or took control of, British settlements near their new fort, Fort Duquesne (doo-KAYN).

The Battle of Jumonville Glen

That year, the British sent 22-year-old George Washington, in command of a group of men, to push the French out. More than 10 French soldiers and one British soldier died. In May 1754, French and British forces met in the Battle of Jumonville Glen in Pennsylvania.

George Washington

Learn More

At the Battle of Fort Necessity in July 1754, Washington was forced to surrender to French forces. The British then sent General Edward Braddock to North America to lead the British forces. He died in battle in 1755.

Native Americans Help

Some of the Native American groups living around the Ohio River valley became **allies** of the Europeans. Many different Native American groups allied with the French. The Iroquois Confederacy, a large, strong group in New York, fought with the British.

Native American allies arrive at a French camp.

Learn More

The French and Indian War got part of its name from the number of Native Americans who took part. The Native peoples wanted control of their own land. They fought for the side they thought would win.

The Seven Years' War

The French and Indian War was a part of a larger war. The European part of the war began in 1756, when Austria tried to reclaim land in Europe. Today, this war is called the Seven Years' War. At first, France won many battles.

The French army celebrates a victory.

Learn More

During the Seven Years' War, France and Great Britain also fought over areas they had claimed in India.

For a time, the fighting in North America slowed because of the Seven Years' War in Europe. By the late 1750s, though, the British forces started to claim more **victories**. In 1759, the British captured Fort Carillon at the end of Lake Champlain.

cannon at Fort Ticonderoga

Learn More

After it was captured, the French Fort Carillon was renamed Fort Ticonderoga. "Ticonderoga" comes from the Iroquois word meaning "between two waters."

Capturing Canada

After the British took Fort Carillon, they continued further North. The British moved into what is now Canada and captured Quebec City. Quebec City was built at a part of the St. Lawrence River that gave entry into the rest of New France. The French **surrendered** the city after a battle.

Learn More

Quebec wasn't just protected by the French forces. Because it was built on top of a cliff above the river, Quebec had some natural protection too.

In 1760, the British forces captured the city of Montreal in New France too. The capture of Montreal was the end of the fighting in North America in the French and Indian War. But the fighting continued between France, Great Britain, and their allies in Europe.

Learn More

The Seven Years' War was fought in Europe by many different European countries. North America was mostly affected by the fighting between Great Britain and France.

The Family Compact

Spain and France joined forces to fight the British in 1761. Their agreement was called the Family Compact. This was because the king of France and the king of Spain were cousins. But the French couldn't **recover**. After many losses in Europe, the French sought peace in 1762.

King Charles III of Spain (left) and King Louis XV of France (below)

Learn More

The Family Compact of 1761 was the third Family Compact between Spain and France.

The Treaty of Paris

In 1763, the **Treaty** of Paris officially ended the Seven Years' War and the French and Indian War. Great Britain took control of French Canada. It also now controlled France's land east of Mississippi River and in India, Africa, and the Mediterranean.

This illustration represents the Treaty of Paris. The woman at right hands olive branches of peace to the other parties who represent many countries.

Learn More

Great Britain owed some of its victories to its powerful navy. The Battle of Quiberon Bay off the coast of France was one of Great Britain's biggest victories.

Spain also gained land from the Treaty of Paris, including land west of the Mississippi. Even though Great Britain captured Cuba in the war, the treaty returned it to Spain. However, Florida was added to British **territory** in North America.

Caribbean islands

Learn More

France regained the Caribbean islands it lost to Great Britain.

Start of Revolution

The French and Indian War ended in 1763, but that wasn't the end of war in North America. Because wars cost so much money, Great Britain was in **debt**. This led to the British taxing its 13 North American colonies. In part because of this, the American **Revolution** started in 1775.

Learn More

The American colonists believed the British shouldn't be able to directly tax them. Great Britain didn't agree.

Timeline

1750s
Tension over land claims grows between France and Great Britain.

1754
The French build Fort Duquesne. The British and French meet at the Battle of Jumonville Glen.

1756
The Seven Years' War begins.

1759
Great Britain takes Fort Carillon and then Quebec City after invading Canada.

1760
Montreal is captured by the British. Fighting ends in North America.

1761
Spain and France sign the Family Compact to join forces against the British.

1763
The Treaty of Paris is signed in Paris, France. This ends the Seven Years' War and the French and Indian War.

Glossary

ally: One of two or more people or groups who work together.

colony: A piece of land under the control of another country.

debt: The state of owing money.

fort: A building or set of buildings made especially strong to house troops or aid travelers.

recover: To return to a normal state after a hard time.

revolution: A movement to overthrow an established government.

surrender: To give up.

tension: A state of anger between groups.

territory: An area of land that a group of people consider to be their own and will fight to defend.

treaty: An agreement between countries.

victory: A win over an opponent.

For More Information

Books

Forbes, Megan. *Major Events in American History*. Berkeley, CA: Rockridge Press, 2021.

Katirgis, Jane, and Tracie Egan. *Meet George Washington: America's First President*. New York, NY: Enslow Publishing, 2020.

Website

Britannica Kids: French and Indian War
kids.britannica.com/kids/article/French-and-Indian-War/353151
Learn more about why this war was fought.

Publisher's note to educators and parents: *Our editors have carefully reviewed this website to ensure that it is suitable for students. Many websites change frequently, however, and we cannot guarantee that a site's future contents will continue to meet our high standards of quality and educational value. Be advised that students should be closely supervised whenever they access the internet.*

Index

American Revolution, 28
Canada, 6, 18, 24, 30
Family Compact of 1761, 22, 23, 30
Fort Carillon (Ticonderoga), 16, 17, 18, 30
Fort Duquesne, 8, 9, 30
France, 4, 6, 8, 9, 10, 11, 12, 14, 15, 18, 20, 21, 22, 23, 24, 27, 30
Great Britain, 4, 6, 8, 9, 10, 11, 12, 15, 16, 18, 20, 21, 22, 24, 25, 26, 27, 28, 29, 30
Native Americans, 5, 12, 13
Seven Years' War, 14, 16, 21, 24, 30
Spain, 4, 7, 22, 23, 26, 30
13 colonies, 6, 8, 28, 29
Treaty of Paris, 24, 26, 30
Washington, George, 10, 11